# WE WERE HERE FIRST
## THE NATIVE AMERICANS

# THE
# COMANCHE

Russell Roberts

PURPLE TOAD
PUBLISHING

Printing  1  2  3  4  5  6  7  8  9

Publisher's Cataloging-in-Publication Data
Roberts, Russell.
  The Comanche / written by Russell Roberts.
    p. cm.
    Includes bibliographic references and index.
      ISBN 9781624691607
1. Comanche Indians—Juvenile literature. I.
Series: We were here first.
  E99.C85 2016
  978.004/9745

Library of Congress Control Number: 2015941836

eBook ISBN: 9781624691614

# CONTENTS

The Comanches were one of the most aggressive of Native American tribes.

# CHAPTER 1
## KIDNAPPED!

It was the morning of May 19, 1836, on the Texas plains. The Parker family and others who lived in the tiny outpost of Parker's Fort were hard at work in the fields outside the 12-foot-high-log stockade fence that surrounded the settlement.

Suddenly, the peaceful morning exploded into a frenzy of screams, blood, and confusion as hundreds of Comanches and other Native Americans attacked! Bullets and arrows whistled through the air, mixing with the screams of women and children and the shouts of men. A woman and young child looked up to see a Comanche bearing down on them . . .

Less than a month before, on April 21, Sam Houston and his rag-tag army of Texas volunteers had defeated the Mexican Army under Santa Anna at the Battle of San Jacinto, just 120 miles south. The victory freed Texas from the rule of Mexico and established its independence.

The people in Texas rejoiced at the news. Santa Anna and his army had cut a vicious swath of death and destruction through Texas since coming up from Mexico earlier in the year

**A wounded Sam Houston receives the captured Santa Anna, who had fled the fighting at San Jacinto and tried to disguise himself in the uniform of an ordinary soldier to avoid being recognized.**

to squash the settlers' independence movement. At San Antonio de Bexar, he had conquered the Alamo and killed all the Texicans (white settlers living in Mexican Texas) defending it on March 6. Santa Anna continued on, determined to crush the rebellion and punish those who opposed him.

Houston's victory at San Jacinto had changed everything. Like many of the people who lived in Texas, the Parkers had emigrated there from the United States, eager for a fresh start in a new country. Now that Texas had gained its independence, that fresh start was assured; the approximately 40 men, women, and children of Parker's Fort could get on with the business of living.[1] So it was that they were planting corn that they would certainly need for food during the coming winter when suddenly a group of Indian warriors on horseback appeared. Most of the Indians were Comanches—the fiercest tribe on the Southern Plains.

Parker's Fort

Parker's Fort was located near the Navasota River in west Texas, about 40 miles east of present-day Waco, Texas. It was isolated, far away from protection by other settlements, and vulnerable to attack. Parker's Fort was deep inside Comanche territory. Rumors had swirled that the Indians were planning on attacking, but the people of Parker's Fort had little choice but to plant then or risk not having enough food for the winter. Still, things had been quiet; the Parkers, although they carried their single-shot rifles with them out to the fields, left the stockade's main gate open for convenience, not fearing an attack.

So it was surprising when the large group of Indians—estimated at anywhere from 500 to 800—showed up that May morning.[2] Waving a white flag, two of them rode out ahead of the rest. Unarmed, Benjamin Parker walked over and asked what they wanted. He came back and told his brother that the Indians were asking for a steer to eat and directions to a waterhole. He didn't believe them, he said, but he was going back to talk with them once more.

Sadly, Benjamin's instincts had been right. When he returned to the Indians, they surrounded him, clubbed him to the ground, and stabbed him repeatedly with their lances. Then, with a piercing cry, they rushed for the fort's open gate.

Benjamin's niece, Rachael Plummer, watched as the Indians killed her uncle. She tried to run for safety with her son, 18-month-old James Pratt, in her arms. The Indians cut her off, then beat her over the head with a hoe until she let the boy go. ". . . the first I recollect, they were dragging me along by the hair. I made several unsuccessful attempts to raise to my feet before I could do it," she later said.[3] She saw an Indian warrior carry away her little boy, who was helplessly screaming, "Mother, oh Mother!"[4]

Comanches on horseback were a superb fighting force, and difficult to fight or defend against.

Silas Parker got off one shot before he was killed. Samuel Frost and his teenage son Robert were also killed. John Parker was killed and so was his wife Sally. The Indians rampaged through the stockade, ripping apart books, smashing bottles, and tearing apart mattresses.

The Comanches then galloped away with their captives—Rachael and her son James, another young woman named Elizabeth Kellogg, and two of Silas Parker's children, eight-year-old John and nine-year-old Cynthia Ann Parker.

Although no one suspected it that day, the attack on Parker's Fort and the kidnapping of Cynthia Ann Parker would become one of the most infamous in Texan—and American—history.

# The Searchers

A scene from the film *The Searchers,* when Ethan Edwards (John Wayne) finally recovers his long-kidnapped niece (Natalie Wood).

The kidnapping of little Cynthia Ann Parker was the basis for one of the greatest American movies ever made: *The Searchers*. The movie starred John Wayne and was directed by John Ford.

The film's plot concerns the search, over many years, by Ethan Edwards (played by Wayne) for his young niece, who was kidnapped by Comanches who raided his brother's farm and killed his brother, wife, and son. Just like the actual search for Cynthia Ann Parker, the search by Wayne and co-star Jeffrey Hunter takes many years. Wayne's character is a racist with a deep hatred of Indians, and one of the film's themes is racism. Central to the story is the belief that once white children have lived among Native Americans and adopted their ways they can no longer thrive in white society. Wayne's character begins to question whether he will want to kill his niece because of it.

Released in 1956, *The Searchers* is considered a cinematic classic. In 2007, the American Film Institute ranked it 12th on its list of the 100 greatest American movies of all time.

It is believed that at one time, Comanches were part of the Shoshone people, whose name comes from a Shoshone word meaning "high-growing grasses."

# CHAPTER 2
## ANYONE WHO WANTS TO FIGHT ME ALL THE TIME

For centuries, the Comanches were the masters of the Southern Great Plains. However, they did not originally come from that area. Many historians believe that the Comanches were once part of the Shoshone people, who lived along the upper Platte River in what is now Wyoming. Sometime before 1700, the group that became the Comanches started moving south from Wyoming.

There are several possible reasons why the group of Comanches broke off from the Shoshones and went south. One is that the Comanches separated from the others because of the death of a boy in a children's game. Another is that two powerful warriors got into a bitter dispute over how to divide a bear carcass.

The usefulness of the horse played a major role in the decision to leave the mountains. Horses had initially been let loose on the Great Plains by Spaniards in the late 17th century. It is likely that small groups of Shoshones captured some wild horses, went out hunting buffalo on them, and realized the advantages that this method had over hunting on foot. It was far easier to move to where millions of buffalo were—the Great Plains—rather than drag the buffalo meat back to a far-

> **The Comanches were expert horsemen, who could not only could ride better than just about anyone, but also raised their own horses.**

away camp. So, over time, those who chose to left the Wyoming mountains for the Great Plains.

The Comanches became not just horse riders, but also horse experts. They learned how to breed them better than any other Native American tribe. By the 19th century, the Comanches had vast horse herds; one band of 2,000 Comanches owned 15,000 horses.[1]

The Comanches became the finest horsemen. One popular opinion held that while other Indian tribes rode horses, the Comanches lived on horseback. Thanks to their invention of a leather thong slipped over a horse's neck, a Comanche could hang over the animal's side while riding, shielding himself from arrows or bullets.

The Comanches' mastery of horses made them the ultimate nomads. They were always on the move, following the buffalo herds. Unlike other Native American tribes, the Comanches built no buildings or structures that they could not disassemble overnight, load onto a travois (type of sled) strapped to a horse or dog, and move somewhere else.

"The Comanches constitute the largest and most terrible nomadic nation anywhere in the territory of the Mexican republic," wrote French naturalist Jean-Louis Berlandier in the late 1820s, when the Southwest was part of Mexico. "The extremes of the weather and the privations [hardships] of a life of constant turmoil combine to give them a physical hardiness peculiarly their own."[2]

The word "Comanche" may have several different origins. In 1705, the Spanish first made contact with the Comanches when they encountered a group of Ute Indians traveling with another group that they did not recognize. The Utes said their companions were *Koh-mahts,* meaning "Those Who are Always Against Us." The Spanish wrote this down as *Komántcia,* which then was also written as *Comantz* and *Commanche.* Eventually, the word became standardized as *Comanche.*[3]

Other possible meanings of the Ute word "komantcia" are "my adversary" or "anyone who wants to fight me all the time."[4] The Comanches referred to themselves as "Nemernuh" meaning "The People."[5]

There was not one large tribe of Native Americans called Comanches. Rather, there were approximately 12 groups—known as "bands"—that made up the Comanche nation. These bands spoke the same language and knew that they were related, even though they lived with different groups of people. Some of the more prominent Comanche bands were the Penateka (Honey Eaters), who lived in central and southern Texas; the Nokoni (Those Who Turn Back) from northeast Texas; the Quahadi (Antelope Eaters) from northwest Texas and New Mexico; the Yamparika (Root Eaters) who inhabited western Kansas and southeastern Colorado; and the Kotsotekas (Buffalo Eaters), found near the Arkansas river. There was even a Comanche band called the Jupes (People of the Timber) that lived in southern Colorado.

Since Comanche bands could be separated by hundreds of miles, there was not one leader who spoke for all Comanches. Occasionally, however, one individual of extraordinary ability emerged and was able to effectively represent a large group of Comanches. One such leader was named

Ecueracapa, who was said to represent 600 Comanche villages in the western Texas/New Mexico region in the late 18th century.[6] In 1786, thanks to Ecueracapa, peace was made between the Comanches and the Spanish that lasted for many years.

However, peace for the Comanches was the exception, rather than the rule. Writer Glenn Frankel points out that modern depictions of Native Americans in books and film often show them seeking harmony with Nature and suffering from white settlers

Comanche braves

intruding on their land, but this was not always true for the Comanches. ". . . the Comanches were nobody's victims and no one's friends," Frankel writes. "They were magnificent, brutal, and relentless."[7]

This "brutal and ruthless" tribe had kidnapped two women and three children from Parkers' Fort and taken them into a desolate, foreboding region that they ruled, but which few others could survive in—a vast territory known as Comancheria.

Was there any hope for the captives?

A Comanche and his horse were like two beings with a single brain, each acting together no matter what the circumstances.

As the Europeans found out, it was nearly impossible to defeat Comanches on horseback.

Mounted Comanches raced toward their enemy in no particular formation. Instead they came forward as a galloping, swirling mass of riders in a confusing cloud of dust, weaving back and forth and in and out at lightning speed, presenting targets that were there one second, and gone the next. European troops were used to shooting at massed groups of approaching soldiers. This didn't work against the darting and weaving Comanches. For this same reason, cannon were also ineffective against attacking Comanches on horseback.

Another favorite warfare tactic of European soldiers was charging the enemy, but again this proved useless against Comanches. They never stood still to receive an enemy's charge. Comanche horses were quick and agile compared to the heavier European horses, and they could instantly dart away from an oncoming foe.

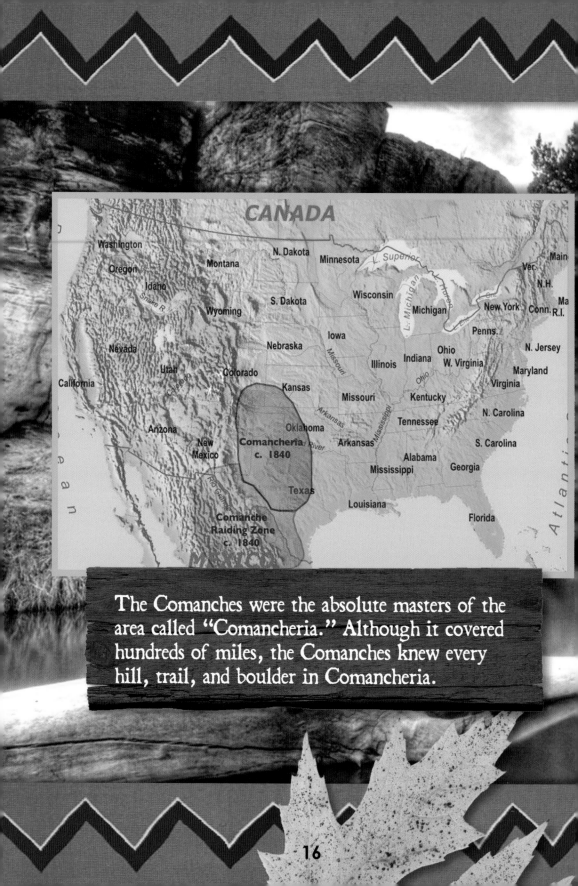

The Comanches were the absolute masters of the area called "Comancheria." Although it covered hundreds of miles, the Comanches knew every hill, trail, and boulder in Comancheria.

# CHAPTER 3
## COMANCHERIA AND THE THIRST FOR WAR

*Comancheria*—the Comanche territory—was a region of hundreds of miles that encompassed parts of five future American states.

Comancheria was an egg-shaped territory that sprawled from present-day southern Colorado through western and central Oklahoma, southwestern Kansas, and eastern New Mexico. It also included a good portion of central and northern Texas, from San Antonio north, including the entire Texas Panhandle.

Before the Comanches arrived, this area had been the domain of the Apaches. However, even the tough and determined Apaches were no match for the mounted Comanches. Apaches who farmed found themselves easy prey for the Comanches, who would race through their fields destroying crops, and roar through their villages like a whirlwind, destroying everything and taking women and children captive. Since the Comanches moved often, the Apaches found it difficult to locate them to fight back. The Apaches began to be systematically destroyed as a people by the Comanches; running away was their only option. By 1725, the Apaches had fled from their former lands in Texas into the Southwest (the present-day states of New Mexico and Arizona).

Comancheria was a vast land of dusty trails and large boulders, of long, waving grasses, occasional streams, and pock-marked by hidden canyons and hills. During the spring rainy season, wildflowers bloomed all over, green grass shimmered in the wind, and small lakes formed. Then the rains ceased and the relentless summer sun baked the ground, drying out the lakes, killing the flowers, and browning the grass. The winters were often mild, and soon the returning rains began Nature's cycle all over again.

Comancheria contained vast buffalo herds numbering in the millions that moved like a giant brown tide, ebbing and flowing back and forth across the land. Besides the buffalo, hunting game included pronghorns (similar to antelopes), bears, elk, great cats, hares, and rabbits.

At one time the Great Plains were covered by millions of buffalo, and the Comanches not only hunted them for food but for the many useful products that they provided.

**The Comanches felt so secure in Comancheria that their camps were often established without guards or other security features.**

By 1750, the Comanches were the absolute rulers of Comancheria; few others dared venture into the area.[1] They set up their teepees in family groups alongside rivers, sometimes for as long as 15 miles, with no security precautions. So, ironically, the camps of the most feared warriors on the Great Plains were also the most vulnerable to enemy attack. The trick was getting to the camps in the first place.

The war against the Apaches changed Comanche culture. It made war desirable, and they became dissatisfied with buffalo hunting as the focal point of their existence.[2]

Because of the importance of war, Comanche men mainly gained prestige by leading others in battle. "A Comanche band at peace was composed of males without purpose . . ." said historian T. R. Fehrenbach.[3] The self-image of an ideal Comanche male was that of a fierce, combative warrior. A boy became a man through aggressive warrior activity, and he remained so only by continually demonstrating these skills. Any sign of weakness was not tolerated.

> In the Comanche culture, being recognized as a brave warrior was the highest honor possible, and each fighter tried his best to achieve that goal.

Because of this, the process of aging was dreaded by Comanches because aging diminished their warrior skills. "The brave die young" became a common saying among them.[4]

The Comanche war process was an elaborate one. The first step was for a warrior to convince others that he had made powerful medicine. If he convinced the others, then he became the war chief, and the others on the war party agreed to follow his orders. Warriors decided to take part in the campaign or not depending upon their own individual feelings and their confidence in their own medicine.

Next, an elaborate dance was held in camp to honor and excite the warriors. Women acted as cheerleaders during the dance, encouraging the warriors by dancing, shrieking, and crying.

The war party painted their faces black—the color of death—and left camp, always at night. However, because the warriors were exhausted by the dance ceremony, they often went only a short distance before making camp.

The Comanche war party moved stealthily across the land, reading signs that others ignored, such as a broken branch, footprints, or campfire ashes. It was something that only people who lived out in the open could do. During the day, they usually remained hidden within rocky canyons or in the woods. The idea was to secretly arrive at the enemy's location, and swoop down on them unexpectedly.

The Comanches followed a practice in warfare called counting coup. This meant racing up to a living enemy and either touching him or landing a blow from a knife or spear. This took great courage and was a large risk. A

**When in battle, the Comanches followed a practice called "counting coup," which meant to touch an enemy and/or wound him with a spear or knife and was considered an act of extraordinary bravery.**

warrior who struck a blow on an enemy in battle would immediately scream *"Aaa-hey"!* This meant "I claim it," meaning he claimed coup against that enemy. Coup needed to be seen by others, so the cry was more a plea for recognition rather than a yell of triumph. The more coup a warrior had, the greater respect he was given.[5]

During warfare, Comanches also tried to kill their enemies. However, it was important to the Comanches to take captives, like the women and children taken from Parkers' Fort.

But why?

**Captives were often treated harshly by the Comanches, particularly in the beginning after just being taken prisoner.**

# Houston's Failed Attempt

Unlike many frontier leaders, Sam Houston was sympathetic toward Native Americans. In the early 1830s, he had lived with the Cherokee Indians. He married a Cherokee woman named Tiana Rogers in 1830, and visited Washington D.C. to lobby politically for the Cherokees.

So when Houston became leader of the new nation of Texas (it did not become a U.S. state until 1845), he tried hard to bring peace between whites and Comanches. However, in return for peace, the Comanches wanted to know precisely which land the whites wanted. Chief Muguara of the Penateka Comanches said whites would be left alone if ". . . they would just draw a line

Sam Houston in 1861

showing what land they claim, and keep on their side of it."[6]

This Houston could not do. Texans wanted to go where they wanted, when they wanted, without restriction. Houston's peace efforts were ultimately unsuccessful. "If I built a high wall between the red men and the white, the whites would scheme day and night to find a way around it," Houston said ruefully.[7]

A typical Comanche family could contain more than one wife, the family's natural children, and any captives that had been taken.

# CHAPTER 4
# A COMANCHE WOMAN'S WORK WAS NEVER DONE

The Comanches lived in a male-dominated society. Men did the hunting and fighting, while women did the rest of the work around camp. They would start their duties early in the morning, lacing their infants into cradle boards, then strapping the cradle boards to their backs, and setting to work. Comanche women would carry wood and water into camp, prepare and cook food, either set up or take down teepees, and perform many other tasks.

A Comanche man could have more than one wife. The wives of strong men—those who were respected hunters and leaders in battle—were envied and admired by multiple Comanche women. It was easier for women to live in households with multiple wives, because it cut down on their heavy workloads. One woman was always the "top wife," with the others below her in rank. Newer wives often became targets of abuse by older, established wives. Sadly, the husband more often than not would pretend not to notice these obvious rivalries (Comanche men sometimes attempted to steal other men's wives, but never their horses).

Comanche families were usually small. A family larger than three people was unusual. Some historians have speculated

Comanche mothers simply strapped their babies
to their backs and continued performing their
many chores.

that the large amount of time Comanche women spent on horseback
caused them to have many miscarriages, thus contributing the tribe's low
birth rate.[1]

Children were welcomed by the Comanches. During childbirth, the
husband was forbidden to be anywhere close to his wife. Midwives helped
with births. If there was a grandfather, he waited outside the teepee during
the birthing process. Once the baby was born, the husband was either told,
"You have a close friend"—meaning that the baby was a boy—or merely,
"It is a girl." The birth of twins was considered an unlucky omen.

Since parents were far too busy with everyday chores and tasks, training
children usually fell to grandparents and/or aunts and uncles. Thus, fathers

and mothers never had to discipline their children. Comanche parents loved their children intensely and indulged them whenever possible.

Since Comanche women had such hard lives full of toil, their men frequently took captives to assist the women with their work. Before there were American settlers in the southern Plains, many Comanche captives came from small villages in Northern Mexico that were easy targets. One estimate suggests that the number of captives was about 2,000 by the early 1800s.[2]

Captives were often treated brutally, at least in the beginning. Rachael Plummer said that, as she lay tightly tied on the first night of her abduction, another captive called to her and she answered her. In response, the Comanches jumped on both of the women so hard that it nearly killed them. Later that night the prisoners were kicked and stomped on.

The anger and resentment some Native Americans felt toward whites would often surface in violent ways, like the warriors' treatment of the prisoners shown above. The Comanches were no exception.

Being taken captive by Comanches was a frightening possibility for every pioneer woman on the southern Great Plains—a possibility that sometimes came true.

Plummer was eventually placed with a family consisting of a man, woman, and daughter. Her duties around camp included tanning buffalo skins and tending to the needs of the horses.

Adult female captives were not well treated by the Comanches, and Plummer was often subject to beatings. The Indians could be incredibly cruel, yet they also admired bravery. One day, Plummer fought the Comanche girl from her family while others looked on. They did not interfere or punish Plummer because they felt that she showed courage. Following the fight, she became known as "the fighting squaw."[3]

Comanches had other reasons for taking captives besides the need for labor. Trading or ransoming captives for food, clothing, and other goods became part of their economy. To them, it was like trading any other commodity.

Another reason for taking prisoners, particularly young boys and girls between ages 6 and 12, was to help increase the tribe's numbers. These children were given to Comanche families that had lost children of their own. The families treated the new additions as their own, showering the children with kindness and affection. These children usually quickly absorbed Comanche culture. Gradually, they would become as Comanche as anyone born into the tribe.

A ten-year-old captive girl named Bianca Babb wrote about her new life as a Comanche. On cold nights, her Comanche mother, named Tekwashna, would stand Bianca in front of the fire and slowly turn her around until she was warm, then carefully wrap her in buffalo robes. She taught her to swim, and both would jump into the river and play together. Tekwashna made her clothing, and Bianca was renamed Tijana, meaning "Texas." Other Comanche children came to play with her and tried to make her feel welcome.

"Every day," Babb said, "seemed to be a holiday."[4]

Some Comanche captives, mainly children such as 10-year-old Bianca Babb, had pleasurable memories of their time spent with Comanche families.

Life in a Comanche village was one of constant work for women, who were responsible for many tasks, including putting up and taking down teepees.

Another captive boy lived with a Comanche family for several years until ransomed. Later, writing about the day he was to leave, he said, "Their kindness to me had been lavish and unvarying . . . I could scarcely restrain my emotions when the time came for the final goodbye."[5]

# All Parts of the Buffalo

**Buffalo hunt**

All parts of a buffalo were used by the Comanches.

The stomach and intestines were cleaned, filled with meat, then roasted for food. The tongue and liver were also eaten. The front shoulders were cut into thin slices, dried, and turned into jerky. The stomach lining was used to carry water or to cook food in. The bladder was inflated with air, which then was used as a water canteen or for food storage. The sinews were used for thread, straps, or string. The horn sheaths were used as cups for drinking. After the hide was dried, it was tanned and then made into clothing, a teepee cover, blanket, or robe. The animal's brains were mixed into a paste that was used to both soften and waterproof the hide. The paste was often stomped by foot into the hide, and it could take days for this exhausting work to be completed and for the hide to pass inspection by the Comanche woman in charge.

As more and more settlers streamed into Texas, they pushed farther and farther into Comancheria, disrupting the buffalo and living on land that had formerly been home to the Comanches.

# CHAPTER 5
## THE END OF COMANCHERIA

For years, the Comanches ruled Comancheria. However, in the early 1820s, American settlers began streaming into Texas. Attracted by the Mexican government's offer to settle down and civilize the sparsely-populated region, men like Stephen F. Austin led large groups of Americans desperate for a fresh start into the wide-open spaces of Texas.

Initially, the Comanches had little to fear from these newcomers. The horses the Americans had were mainly work horses; the Comanche horses were swift and used to galloping at high speeds across the ground guided only by the pressure of their riders' knees. The most common weapon the Americans brought to Texas, the Kentucky long rifle, was unsuitable for fighting against a rapidly moving target, like a Comanche warrior on horseback. The rifle was cumbersome to load and virtually useless while riding horseback. By the time a man had managed to fire one shot, an attacking group of Comanches could have shot numerous arrows at him, usually with deadly accuracy.

Thus, the Comanches held all the advantages against these intruders, and probably felt confident that they would run the Americans off their land just as they had done with the Apaches.

First formed in 1823 by Stephen F. Austin, the Texas Rangers became protectors against the Comanches and other Indians who threatened settlers living in the frontier. However, the government had little money or supplies to give to the Rangers, so the men often had to provide their own food (sometimes stealing chickens and hogs from settlers), clothing, horses, and weapons.

However, that mattered little to the men who became rangers. Most of them were young, single, and looking for adventure; fighting Comanches on the open range and living free under the stars was a dream come true.

The fighting between Comanches and settlers intensified when the Texas legislature, over the veto of President Sam Houston, opened the entire republic to settlement. It offered 1,280 free acres to every family including lands that were part of Comancheria. The situation grew worse in late 1838 when Houston was succeeded as president by Mirabeau B. Lamar. He declared that ". . . the white man and the red man cannot dwell in harmony together."[1] He called for war on the Comanches.

The Rangers found themselves in the thick of this war. At first, they suffered from the same disadvantages as the settlers—slower horses and inadequate weapons. However, they soon began to adopt Comanche war tactics, such as riding at night by moonlight and swooping down by surprise on Comanche camps, and soon the Rangers were a match for the Indians. The Comanches called them "those who always follow our trails."[2]

The Rangers did two other things to help them fight the Comanches: They bred lighter, faster horses, and they began using new multi-shot revolvers developed by Samuel Colt. Using these weapons, early in 1840 the Rangers inflicted two severe defeats on large bands of Penateka Comanches.

In March 1840, Penateka Chief Muguara rode into San Antonio along with 65 other Comanche men, women, and children. They had come to meet with Texas officials at the city's Council House to discuss a truce.

The officials had asked the Comanches to bring all their American captives. However, when the Penatekas arrived all they had with them was sixteen-year-old Matilda Lockhart. She had been badly abused and her

**San Antonio Council House and plaza**

condition angered the Texans. When the Indians and Texans came together in the council room and the Texans asked about other captives, Muguara said that they were being held by other bands over which he had no control. He then suggested that the Comanches intended to ransom them back one at a time, as they had always done.

"How do you like that answer?" smirked Muguara.[3]

Already furious about Lockhart's condition, the Texans were not amused by Muguara's comment. Soldiers rushed into the room, and the Comanches were told that they would all be jailed until the other captives were returned.

Suddenly, the small room erupted into a series of shouts, shrieks, and war cries. The Comanches attacked the soldiers, who fired back at them. The room filled with gun smoke. When it cleared, all of the Comanches and several whites were dead.

The remaining Comanches were imprisoned, except for one woman who was told to ride out and tell the other Comanches to bring in all their captives. Instead, the Comanches retaliated by torturing and killing over a dozen captives they had been holding.

35

Soon, the Texas frontier became a place of death for both Native Americans and whites. No road heading to San Antonio was safe to travel. Attacks by both sides became commonplace. In August 1840, a band of 1,000 Comanche warriors attacked the town of Victoria, Texas, then headed to the seaside town of Linnville. While the people watched in terror from boats just offshore, the Comanches burned and pillaged the town. A force of 200 Texas Rangers pursued these Comanches and defeated them at the Battle of Plum Creek.

In 1841, Houston was again elected president of Texas. In 1844, he held a peace conference between the two sides that resulted in mutual vows of friendship and a Comanche pledge not to attack Texas settlements.

**The Battle of Plum Creek was an attempt by Texans to recapture horses and other items taken by Comanche Chief Buffalo Hump and his warriors after their attack on the Texas cities of Victoria and Linnville.**

But the biggest change was yet to come for the Comanches.

In 1845, Texas became part of the United States. That, and the discovery of gold in California a few years later, brought thousands of settlers flooding into Comanche territory, either to live or else pass through on their way to the west coast. They destroyed water holes and disrupted buffalo migration patterns. The result was a loss of the animal so important to the Comanches. Meanwhile, other Texas Indians displaced by white settlement entered Commancheria, competing with Comanches for the dwindling food supply. Food became so scarce that some Comanches had to eat their own horses.

In 1849, the U.S. government built a series of forts in Texas to protect the settlers. This made people feel safer, and they pushed even farther into Comancheria.

However, the worst thing that the whites brought with them was disease. Cholera, smallpox, and other illnesses spread through Comanche camps. Having lived in isolation for so long, the Comanches had no natural defenses against those diseases. One estimate is that in just a few months nearly half of the Penatekas died from disease. Other bands who lived farther north suffered as well.

The days when the Comanches held sway over vast amounts of territory and could roam freely were fast disappearing. The American government began forcing Native Americans all over, including Comanches, onto reservations and made them give up their traditional way of life—hunting— for farming. (Making passive farmers out of the fierce Comanches was no easy task. One chief said that it was like trying to turn a mighty wolf into a dog.)

Squads of Texas Rangers and the U.S. military relentlessly hunted down groups of raiding Indians. On one such occasion, in the autumn of 1860, an attack on a Comanche camp resulted in soldiers capturing a Comanche with blue eyes—Cynthia Ann Parker, who had been taken captive by the Comanches as a child so many years before at Parker's Fort. Reunited with her white family, she tried once to return to her Comanche family, and her life was never really the same. She died in 1870.

After being taken captive by the Comanches as a child and then rescued many years later, Cynthia Ann Parker was never comfortable back in the white world.

The Civil War provided a brief respite for the Comanches. Federal and Texas troops fought each other, and had little time for Indians. The Comanches stayed neutral, and stole horses and supplies from both sides. However, the end of the war in 1865 brought a renewed effort by the U.S. government to end attacks between Indians and whites on the Southern Plains and Texas. Federal troops were ready to protect white settlers, but unwilling to stop the settlement of Comancheria by settlers.

In 1867, the Comanches, Kiowas, and other southern Great Plains tribes met with representatives of the U.S. government at Medicine Lodge Creek in Kansas. The government was determined to force all remaining Native Americans onto reservations. The Indians did not want to agree, but realized that they had little choice in the matter. "You can no more stop this than you can stop the sun or moon . . ." Civil War general William T. Sherman told them.[4]

Reluctantly, the Comanches agreed and signed the treaty. It provided them with a 5,546-acre reservation in present-day Oklahoma—a small fraction of the size Comancheria had once been. It did not contain any of the best hunting land, which was in Texas.

Some Comanches refused to go to the reservation and tried to live as they did before. Among them were the Quahadas, one of whose leaders was Quanah Parker—the son of Cynthia Ann Parker and her Comanche husband Peta Nocona.

Yet, it was becoming increasingly difficult for the Comanches to raid, and hunters with rapid-fire rifles were slaughtering buffalo by the thousands, leaving the Southern Great Plains littered with their carcasses.

It was a desperate time for the Comanches still roaming free, and they did a desperate thing: They listened to a Quahada Comanche named Ishatai, who claimed that he could protect them against white bullets. He urged them to attack the whites. Once they were chased away, he said, the buffalo would return.

In June 1874, a war party of several hundred Quahadas along with Kiowas and Cheyennes attacked a trading post at Adobe Walls that contained just 28 buffalo hunters. The Comanches had the advantage in numbers, but with the same types of guns with which they were destroying the buffalo herds, the hunters shot them down. Ishatai's "magic" did not protect them. "Time and again, with the fury of a whirlwind, the Indians charged

**Adobe Walls Battlefield**

upon the building, only to sustain greater losses than they were able to inflict," said a hunter.[5]

Discouraged by the failure of their attack, and hounded by the U.S. Army, the Comanches began entering the reservation. They were half-starved, ill-clothed, and exhausted.

Quanah Parker and his Quahadas were the last remaining band living outside the reservation. On June 2, 1875. Parker led 400 of his people into Fort Sill, Oklahoma.

Chief Ten Bears of the Comanche spoke at the Medicine Lodge Creek peace treaty conference on October 19, 1867. Knowing his life and the lives of all Comanches would be changed forever he said:

"I was born upon the prairie where the wind blew free, and there was nothing to break the light of the sun. I was born where there were no enclosures, and where everything drew free breath. I want to die there, and not within walls. But it is too late. The white man has the country we loved . . ."[6]

**Chief Ten Bears was known for his poetic speeches, but his words of peace could not get the treaties with the United States that the Comanches deserved.**

# Quanah Parker

Quanah Parker was born in either 1845 or 1852. His mother was the celebrated Cynthia Ann Parker. His father was Chief Peta Nocona. In 1860, Nocona was killed by the Texas Rangers and his mother recaptured, forcing young Quanah to join the Quahada band of the Comanches. He became a leader of the band, and led the Quahadas in resisting giving up their freedom for life on the reservation.

However, after the failed attack on Adobe Walls in 1874, Parker knew that his band could not survive in the wild, and so he led them to Fort Sill in Indian Territory (now Oklahoma) in 1875. While many Comanches had trouble adjusting to reservation life, Parker thrived. In response, the reservation agents named him chief of all the Comanches. Parker was successful in this leadership role. He promoted education for Comanche children, supported the establishment of a Comanche police force, became a successful rancher, counted Theodore Roosevelt as a friend, and became a strong and fierce advocate for his people, never letting them forget their proud heritage. At the time of his death in 1911, he was considered one of the wealthiest Indians in America.

Quanah Parker

1. Instead of just one leader, Comanche groups had a head council composed of several important members that made all the decisions, such as when to go to war and when to hunt.

2. The Comanches offered a piece of their food to the spirits and then bury it in the ground.

3. Comanches smoked a pipe as a way of talking to the spirits.

4. A nomadic people, the Comanches moved from place to place, sometimes covering several hundred miles in a single year.

5. Comanches buried their dead in a crevice on a hill or in a tree.

6. Comanche life was divided up into five sections: Baby, child, adolescent, adult, and elder.

7. Because they moved around so much, the Comanches did not use pottery, because it broke easily.

8. If a pregnant Comanche woman went into labor while her band was on the move, she would pause, give birth, rest for a short time, and then catch up to the rest of the group with her baby.

9. Along with other Native American peoples, Comanche code-talkers" helped the United States win World War II.

10. Today, many Comanches live in Oklahoma in the United States.

## Chapter One

1. Glenn Frankel, *The Searchers,* (New York: Bloomsbury, 2013), p. 20.
2. Bill Neeley, *The Last Comanche Chief,* (New York: John Wiley & Sons, 1995), p. 4.
3. Ibid, p. 7.
4. Frankel, p. 23.

## Chapter Two

1. T.R. Fehrenbach, *Comanches,* (New York: Alfred A. Knopf, 1974), p. 94.
2. Glenn Frankel, *The Searchers,* (New York: Bloomsbury, 2013), p. 32.
3. Fehrenbach, p. 90.
4. Morris W. Foster, *Being Comanche*, (Tuscon, AZ: The University of Arizona Press, 1991), p. 36.
5. Frankel, p. 31.
6. *The American Heritage Book of Indians,* Alvin M. Joseph, Jr., editor, (American Heritage Publishing Co., Inc., 1961), p. 378.
7. Frankel, p. 32.

## Chapter Three

1. T.R. Fehrenbach, *Comanches,* (New York: Alfred A. Knopf, 1974), p. 146.
2. Ibid.
3. Ibid, p. 147.
4. Ibid, p. 149.

5. Ibid, p. 76.
6. *Tribes of the Southern Plains,* Henry Woodhead, editor, (Alexandria, VA: Time-Life Books, 1995), p. 132.
7. Fehrenbach, p. 349.

## Chapter Four

1. T.R. Fehrenbach, *Comanches,* (New York: Alfred A. Knopf, 1974), p. 97.
2. Glenn Frankel, *The Searchers,* (New York: Bloomsbury, 2013), p. 39.
3. Bill Neeley, *The Last Comanche Chief,* (New York: John Wiley & Sons, 1995), p. 10.
4. Frankel, p. 44.
5. Neeley, p. 11.

## Chapter Five

1. *Tribes of the Southern Plains,* Henry Woodhead, editor, (Alexandria, VA: Time-Life Books, 1995), p. 132.
2. Ibid, p. 134.
3. Bill Neeley, *The Last Comanche Chief,* (New York: John Wiley & Sons, 1995), p. 26.
4. *Tribes of the Southern Plains,* p. 157.
5. Neeley, p. 96.
6. Chief Ten Bears, http://www.comanchelodge.com/speech.htm

## Books

Cunningham, Kevin, and Peter Benoit. *The Comanche.* Danbury, CT: Scholastic Library Publications, 2011.

Dwyer, Helen, and D.L. Birchfield. *Comanche History and Culture.* New York: Gareth Stevens Publishing, 2012.

Kissock, Heather. *Comanche.* New York: Weigl Pub. Inc., 2010.

Miller, Brandon Marie. *Women of the Frontier: 16 Tales of Trailblazing, Homesteaders, Entrepreneurs, and Rabble-Rousers.* Chicago: Chicago Review Press, 2013.

Sanford, William R. *Comanche Chief Quanah Parker.* New York: Enslow Publications, Inc., 2013.

Schach, David. *Comanche Warriors.* Minneapolis: Bellwether Media, 2011.

## Works Consulted

*The American Heritage Book of Indians,* Alvin M. Joseph, Jr., editor. American Heritage Publishing Co., Inc., 1961.

Brown, Dee. *The American West.* New York: Charles Scribner's Sons, 1994.

Fehrenbach, T.R. *Comanches.* New York: Alfred A. Knopf, 1974.

Foster, Morris W. *Being Comanche.* Tucson, AZ: The University of Arizona Press, 1991.

Frankel, Glenn. *The Searchers.* New York: Bloomsbury, 2013.

*The Native Americans,* Betty Ballantine and Ian Ballantine, editors. Atlanta: Turner Publishing, Inc., 1993.

Neeley, Bill. *The Last Comanche Chief.* New York: John Wiley & Sons, 1995.

Treuer, Anton. *Atlas of Indian Nations.* Washington, DC: National Geographic Society, 2013.

*Tribes of the Southern Plains,* Henry Woodhead, editor. Alexandria, VA: Time-Life Books, 1995.

## On the Internet

Chief Ten Bears

    http://www.comanchelodge.com/speech.htm

Comanche Indians

    http://www.indians.org/articles/comanche-indians.html

Comanche Language

    http://www.native-languages.org/comanche.htm

Native American Facts for Kids

    http://www.bigorrin.org/comanche_kids.htm

Native American Legends

    http://www.legendsofamerica.com/na-commanche.html

Quanah Parker

    http://www.tshaonline.org/handbook/online/articles/fpa28

The Rise and Fall of the Comanche Empire

    http://www.npr.org/2011/05/20/136438816/
    the-rise-and-fall-of-the-comanche-empire

The Texas Comanches

    http://www.texasindians.com/comanche.htm

**Agile** (AA-juhl)—Able to move quickly and easily.

**Commodity** (kuh-MAA-dih-tee)—An article of trade.

**Cumbersome** (KUHM-ber-sum)—Clumsy.

**Depict** (dih-PIKT)—To represent.

**Domain** (doh-MAYN)—Territory governed by a single ruler.

**Ebb**—Flowing back of the tide as the water returns to the sea.

**Emigrate** (EH-mih-grayt)—Leave one region and settle in another.

**Foe** (FOH)—Enemy.

**Mutilate** (MYOO-tih-layt)—Disfigure.

**Pillage** (PILL-ij)—To strip away money and goods by violence.

**Respite** (RES-pit)—Delay for a time.

**Rue** (ROO)—Bitterly regret.

**Sinew** (SIN-yoo)—Tendon.

**Stockade** (STAH-kayd)—An enclosure made with posts and stakes.

**Swath**—To make a display and attract notice.

**Tactic** (TAK-tik)—A plan used to provide an end result.

**Thong** (THAWNG)—A strip of material, often of leather.

**Travois** (truh-VOY)—A device for transporting things, made of two poles joined by a frame.

**Vast**—Immense.

# MEET THE
# AUTHOR

**Rusty**

Russell Roberts has researched, written, and published numerous books for both children and adults. Among his books for adults are *Down the Jersey Shore, Historical Photos of New Jersey*, and *Ten Days to A Sharper Memory*. He has written over 50 nonfiction books for children. Roberts often speaks on the subjects of his books before various groups and organizations. He lives in New Jersey.